Love and Death
in the
Kingdom of Swaziland

Other Books by Glenn Alan Cheney

Ex Cathedra: Stories by Machado de Assis

Be Revolutionary! Some Thoughts from Pope Francis

*Promised Land: A Nun's Struggle to Resist Landlessness,
Lawlessness, Slavery, Poverty, Corruption, Injustice, and
Environmental Catastrophe in Amazonia*

*How a Nation Grieves:
Press Accounts of the Death of Lincoln, the Hunt for Booth,
and America in Mourning*

Thanksgiving: The Pilgrims' First Year in America

*Dr. Jamoke's Little Book of Hitherto Uncompiled
Facts and Curiosities about Bees*

*Journey on the Estrada Real:
Encounters in the Mountains of Brazil*

Journey to Chernobyl: Encounters in a Radioactive Zone

Frankenstein on the Cusp of Something

Passion in an Improper Place

*They Never Knew:
The Victims of Atomic Testing*

Acts of Ineffable Love: Stories by Glenn Cheney

Love and Death in the Kingdom of Swaziland
by Glenn Alan Cheney
with a Foreword by
Sr. Barbara Staley, MSC

Published by
New London Librarium
P.O. Box 248
Hanover, CT 06350
www.NLLibrarium.com

Printed in the United States of America

New London Librarium also published this title as a digital edition, with photographs, in 2012.

ISBN:
Paperback 978-0-9856284-1-3
ePub ISBN: 978-0-9856284-0-6

for

Ana Maria and Speranza

Love and Death
in the
Kingdom of Swaziland

Glenn Alan Cheney

with a Foreword by

Sr. Barbara Staley, MSC

New London Librarium

Contents

Foreword

At first glance this small book may appear as a tribute to two sisters working in Swaziland. But the story is much bigger than that. It is a story of faith. It is a story of Love. A story of what motivates two women to struggle against the odds and find meaningful responses in order to better the lives of the people they serve. It is a story of two women working within their personal limitations to be the hands, to be the feet, to be the heart of Christ here on Earth today.

Women religious throughout the world are spending their lives daily to bring "the joy of the Gospel" (Pope Francis, 2013) to the poor and disenfranchised of the world. Where you find the hungry you will find a Catholic Sister feeding people. Where there is ignorance you will find a Sister educating people. Where there is an orphan you find a religious Sister nurturing that child. Where there are naked people, a sister can be found providing clothes. The mission of all Sisters is to bear the love of Christ to the world by loving Christ in their neighbors and being a voice of and a life of witness against human injustices.

The Missionary Sisters of the Sacred Heart, a congregation founded by St. Frances Cabrini in 1880, is grateful to the author for telling the story of MSC efforts in Swaziland, a country beset by the world's most intense epidemic of HIV and all the consequent social problems. This is just one of many other such stories of MSCs who, today, are active in fifteen countries on six continents. In their ceaseless efforts and undying dedication, they are among the people who still live the mystery of a life for others. People in all nations and of all beliefs still need saints who walk among them. It is encouraging to see MSCs today who incarnate the enthusiasm of Mother Cabrini, who desired to love all peoples in a "too small a world," (Mother Cabrini, retreat notes) and who worked untiringly on behalf of others.

It is my desire that this book helps the reader to know Love and will encourage each in their own lives to share that Love with others.

SR. BARBARA STALEY, MSC
Superior General
Missionary Sisters of the Sacred Heart of Jesus
mothercabrini.org
msccabrini.org
Cabriniministries.org

Prologue

Once upon a time in the Kingdom of Swaziland, life was as good as it was going to get. The folk in the country lived in little round houses of mud, sticks, and reeds. They planted gardens and let their cattle wander around. The folk in the city found jobs, ate imported food, drove imported cars on paved highways. On Sundays, they went to church. They laughed a lot. They drank the tap water. In February, everybody got drunk on home-brewed amarula fruit hootch. In the rainy season, it rained. In August, everybody watched bare-breasted maidens perform the annual reed dance. The king would be there, perhaps to pick another wife. The Swazi culture, millennia old, kept everyone knitted together in a handful of vast families. Orphans were genealogically impossible.

They had their unspeakable side: black magic, witch doctors, social paranoia, chattel-women, abominable sacrifices. They used the same word for love, like, fornicate, and rape. But this culture, dark and bizarre by the standards of the white world, somehow worked to sustain them in a place of thorn bushes, pit vipers, and wars fought with spears and knobkierrie clubs. Seventy percent of the population was rural, and the level of ignorance wasn't advanced much beyond the dark ages. Illiteracy outside a couple of cities was general, beliefs almost prehistoric. Though Protestant and Catholic churches claimed over 80 percent of the population, age-old beliefs ran deep beneath the veneer of Christianity.

For many years Swaziland benefited from the racial nastiness of the neighbor that bordered the kingdom on three sides. When the world refused to do business with the South African apartheid regime, companies from that country set up camp in the little kingdom four hours east of Johannesburg. Though the country was landlocked and without a train line through South Africa or Mozambique to the coast, the economy boomed. King Sobhuza II reaped plenty of revenues and used them not only to take good care of himself, his 70 wives, and his 210 children, but to pass out food, sponsor clinics, support schools, fill potholes, and keep cities livable. He worked with the chiefs of chiefdoms to keep people happy. When he dispensed with the constitution the British colonizers had imposed, no one cared. Everyone loved King Sobhuza.

Sobhuza died in 1982, but his successor, one of many sons, was only 14 years old. Two queen mothers ran the country in succession until the boy turned 18. He was in high school in England when they called him back to be groomed for the throne. In 1986, a week after his eighteenth birthday, he became King Mswati III.

Mswati didn't have much time to learn to be a king. In 1992, drought descended on Swaziland. In 1994, apartheid collapsed, the international boycotts stopped, and the South African companies went home. And then everybody started dying.

The Dust of the Place

Everybody was dying. That was what Sister Ana Maria de Oliveira said on the phone to her province superior, Sister Diane DalleMolle, when she heard that the Missionary Sisters of the Sacred Heart of Jesus, a.k.a. the Cabrini Sisters, were retracting her mission from Swaziland.

"We can't leave now," she pleaded. "Everybody's dying. Everybody." And she started crying. All the babies she and Sister Speranza D'Ambrosi had delivered, educated, raised to adulthood, and trained for a job were all dying. The work of three decades, a whole generation of people, a little impulse of hope for the struggling kingdom, was wasting away.

Sister Ana Maria said, "All we can do is go out to the homesteads and bring them some food and sit with them while they die. Children are everywhere. What are we going to do with all the children?"

Sister Diane had no idea what to do with the children. She was overseeing missions in several countries, from the United States to Australia to Taiwan. That was in 1997. Average life expectancy in Swaziland had already declined from 60-something to 56, and projections

3

were tilting down at a Titanic angle. The sisters of the Sacred Heart had been in Swaziland for 30 years, maintaining a school and convent near Manzini, Swaziland's largest city, and a clinic in the harsh, dusty outback of the Lubombo district, a parish-based outpost called St. Philip's. Things had been going so well in the country that the sisters no longer felt needed. The world had more desperate places.

But then Sister Diane got a call from her General Superior in Rome. She'd heard of the decision to pull out. She said to Diane, "Don't do it."

And Diane asked, "Why not?"

And the Superior General said, "Just don't."

She had grabbed Diane's heart, but her managerial brain needed a reason.

"I can't give you a reason. We just need to stay if we are ever to do the work that God wants us to do. We have to stay in places that seem impossible."

Sister Diane went to see the situation. She flew into Johannesburg, then took a little plane into Swaziland, then took a car an hour down paved roads, then an hour down a bumpy dirt road. She found St. Philip's above the west bank of the Mhlatuze River, which, in the ongoing drought, often barely qualified as a creek. The mission consisted of a few low buildings that housed a little clinic, some staff, the parish priest, an elementary school, and a high school. The church was a dome supported by concrete arches, built, it would seem, to echo sweet Swazi hymns.

And there she found just about everyone dying. Ana Maria took her to some homesteads out among the thorn bushes. The average homestead was a small, circular, wattle-and-daub house with a reed roof. A fence of stick, stones, and thorny branches might surround the place. A few head of cattle and goats might be wandering around the scrub. A scarred and skinny dog might be sleeping in the dust. A few gristly chickens might be scratching around in search of infinitesimal bits of something edible. The houses had little or no furniture or even room for furniture. Rare was the house without at least one person slowly dying on a reed mat on the dirt floor. At one they found three girls lying on mats outside the house. They were 16, 17 and 18, all in the fourth and last stage of AIDS, all infected by the same man. One girl's uterus was distended from her body and covered with fungus. All three had fungal growths around their mouths and down their throats. Their mother was trying to care for them, but there was little she could do.

Cabrini's little clinic didn't have the technical capability to diagnose what the Ana Maria and Speranza knew to be the problem. Even if they could, they had no way to treat HIV/AIDS. Every day more leathery black skeletons staggered in on their spindly knobkierrie staffs. But treatment was superficial at best. The best the sisters could do was alleviate some of the symptoms. The people had to drag themselves back home to die.

And it was time for the sisters to go home, too. Ana Maria was 75, Speranza 85.

Diane wasn't one to walk away from dying people. She had to go back to New York to plead for Swaziland, but something tied her to St. Philip's. As she boarded the little plane to Johannesburg, she was still covered with grit. It was even in her teeth. When she pulled her shoes off to shake them clean, she realized that she loved even the dust of that place.

Back in New York she became more conscious of the oppressive enormity of her job as Provincial Superior. Though a nurse by training, she was overseeing 20 hospitals, clinics, and other institutions. Her congregation's hospital in New York — 1,100 beds, 500 employees — was struggling in the industry's maelstrom of regulations, law suits, restructuring, union demands, technology, AIDS, and soaring costs amid widening poverty. She was spending more in a month than the mission in Swaziland could spend in 20 years. She wanted out, and the outback of Swaziland was about as far out as a Cabrini Sister could get. She wanted to go there, she said, to save her everlasting soul. Her work in New York was God's work, she knew, but it felt like she was walking the other way.

Her board approved an extension of the mission. Ana Maria would go back to her native Brazil, Speranza to New York. Diane would replace them, downshifting, she thought, into a simpler life. She was 61. That was in 2004. Life expectancy in Swaziland had declined to 37 and was still dropping.

But Swaziland wasn't so simple. Instead of lawyers, bankers, union officials, consultants, administrators, and government regulators, she faced plague, drought, corruption, decimated families, legions of orphans, endemic rape, black magic, and ignorance rooted in an impenetrable culture. The government, medieval in its structure and its disregard for its people, obstructed change to any status quo and showed no concern for the well-being of citizens. Dr. Henk Bos had been at St. Philip's for a couple of years. He was the director of laboratories at the Cabrini hospital in Australia. As he handed the mission to Sister Diane, he offered no words of optimism, no illusions of a problem solved or solvable. He told her she would never be able do what she'd come to do, that the problem was impossible to solve. She didn't know what she was doing, didn't know what she'd gotten into. Then he got into the little plane to Johannesburg and flew away.

No Body on Earth But Yours

Diane had second thoughts. They pursued her into bed that night. Lying in the dark of that strange and scary land, she realized that Dr. Hank didn't understand who the Missionary Sisters of Cabrini were, that they had always done what they didn't know how to do, that they didn't surrender to impossibility, not when people were standing in front of them dying.

That disregard for impossibility had always been the history and mission of the MSC. The congregation was founded in 1880 by Frances Cabrini, an Italian woman who didn't let impossibility stand in her way. Dynamic and unstoppable, she founded and secured funding for schools, hospitals, and orphanages in the United States, Nicaragua, Argentina, Brazil, and Europe — all quite impossible for a woman at that period in history, yet she was able to accomplish it. She was canonized in 1946.

The congregation is of sisters rather than nuns, the former tending to go out into the world in with proactive charitable purpose, the latter tending to be cloistered and more focused on prayer. A nun is typically seen in a habit; a sister might well in bib overalls and rubber boots. The

Cabrini sisters have a favorite prayer, a call to action by St. Teresa of Avila: "Christ has no body now on earth but yours, no hands, no feet but yours; yours are the eyes through which he looks with compassion on this world; yours are the feet with which he walks to do good; yours are the hands with which he is to bless men now."

Before they retired from St. Philip's, Ana Maria and Speranza put their hands and compassion together to pull off one more impossibility. They managed to get an orphanage built for 50 children. More precisely defined, it was a hostel, a place where children could stay most of the year. During school breaks they would go back to whoever had last been taking care of them. On the day the hostel opened, 98 children showed up. The sisters put them two to a bed. More showed up the next day. It was a lot of kids to feed, love, and clean up after. The local staff needed a lot of training in the art of raising children. For one thing, they had to learn that beating traumatized children is not the best way to discipline them.

Diane, too, had a lot to learn. She was the only white woman in an area raging with a worsening epidemic. She had one small health clinic staffed with a few Swazi nurses, and she had a hostel with well over a hundred children. She awoke every morning to find people dying on her porch. It was a lot for one woman to handle. She called her Provinceial Superior in New York and asked if Sister Barbara Staley could be assigned to Swaziland. Barbara had a master's degree in social work and had done time in the jungles of Guatemala and the slums of Chicago. She knew how to work with children. She knew how to plan. She knew how to not just get things done but make them get done.

The province superior said no. Diane pleaded with all her heart. When that didn't work, she lied through her teeth. She said she needed Barbara for just three months. She knew perfectly well she was going to keep finding reasons why Barbara couldn't leave. Barbara arrived in late 2004.

Barbara knew how to devise a plan and then execute it, but there was little point in planning anything. As soon as she got off the little plane, she was dealing with immediate problems — the people dying on the porch, the venomous black mamba coiled up in a tree in the back yard, the dilapidated homestead headed by an unprotected prepubescent girl, the car stuck in the river. These problems didn't need plans. They needed immediate attention. Every day, starting well before dawn, Sister Barbara and Sister Diane had to confront the life-and-death urgency of right now.

And they didn't know what they were doing. They had never confronted an epidemic before and certainly had no idea how to treat HIV infection or AIDS. They had no one to advise them on anything. They had no idea how the medical system worked in Swaziland, no idea where to buy food for a hundred-odd children every day, how to train illiterate people, how to run a clinic staffed with nurses who believed black magic worked. They had no time to learn siSwati.

As they started to establish initial measures for dealing with the epidemic, they hit their first inexplicable wall. Everyone was deathly ill, and in most cases it was pretty obvious what the cause was. Step one toward treatment was to have blood tested, yet people were refusing. In fact, the people working with Diane and Barbara refused to even ask people to be tested. Not even nurses would do it. But it made no sense. Though the causes of HIV, from rape to polygamy, held no stigma, having the disease was embarrassing, and asking about it was insulting. The sisters hired Mr. Pius Mamba to provide the language and insight they needed to talk with people. He'd been raised in the rural culture, but he'd always been a Christian and had quite a bit of college education. He went out to the homesteads with the sisters to translate, but he, too, had difficulty asking about testing for HIV. He had to gradually, over the course of half an hour, lead into the question. "Forgive me for being so bold," he'd say. "It isn't me asking this, it's the Sister; she's white, you know...a little crazy; I'm just translating and I need this job, so I have to ask, if you could just try to understand that I don't mean anything by it..." And then all he could do was hope the question didn't lead to a curse that only a witch doctor could remove.

Oddly enough, once the question was asked, the answer was often a desperate yes. So in dark, smoke-filled huts, Diane drew blood. Because of the dim light, the tough muscle tissue of dirt farmers, the dark skin over collapsed veins, she had to use her bare fingers to find a vein and guide the needle in. Then she'd put the blood on ice to take to Good Shepherd Hospital for testing. Sometimes the blood spent the night in plastic bags in the refrigerator back home, in there with the food. It was the only refrigerator they had.

When the test for HIV came back positive, they would have to take the patient to the hospital. They'd be rumbling down unmapped dirt trails by 4:00 a.m. It was the only way to have enough time to pick up Mr. Mamba, find far-flung homesteads, talk people into allowing a blood draw, pick up patients, go to the hospital two hours to the northeast, take blood samples into Manzini for HIV testing, take other samples into the capital, Mbabane, for CD4 testing of white blood cell levels, and then go back to homesteads to inform those who had to go to the hospital the next morning. They packed as many people as they could into an old Toyota Venture, a mini-van modified to hold more passengers than it was built for. It had problems. It was a four-wheel drive vehicle, but only two wheels drove. The battery kept falling out. The lights kept going off. The tires kept going flat. A wheel kept coming off. Not built for off-road travel, the van tended to get stuck in rivers they were driving through, in soft sand, in puddles of dust. On the way to the hospital one night, just after repairs to the electrical system, the lights went out and flames licked out from under the hood. Diane couldn't stop for that. She held a flashlight out the window in case other cars couldn't see the flames coming down the road.

She was a nurse, not a mechanic, and she was at the wheel of a logistical nightmare. She wasn't even much of a driver, either. She didn't know how to drive a standard shift until she got to Swaziland. She didn't know what to do with a battery hanging under the engine, swaying by a cable. She

10

didn't know how to change a flat until Mr. Mamba, who is blind, talked her through it one dark night. She learned to keep a flashlight in the car.

Good Shepherd wasn't much of a hospital. It certainly wasn't up to the challenge of an AIDS epidemic. HIV patients were laid out on the floor of a space not much bigger than a living room. A couple hundred more lay on the ground outside. The only doctor, an American from California, was always angry and shouting, way over his head in patients, dealing with inadequate staff, dispensing inadequate medications, and working with inadequate equipment.

To simply leave patients at Good Shepherd wouldn't be much better than leaving them at home. They were as ignorant as could be, as humble as dirt, unable to understand instructions, afraid to speak up, mystified by the whole medical process. The sisters had to speak for, and think for, their patients. Mr. Mamba said to Sister Barbara, "You care more about these people's lives than they do."

The conditions at homesteads had declined from third-world to sub-human. The sisters came to homesteads so poor that people were walking around naked. They found young children trying to maintain a household while a tubercular parent in the fourth stage of AIDS lay fetid and suppurating on the floor in a cluster of jubilant flies. Water had to come from a river a mile or two or more away, and if the river was dry at that time of year, they'd have to dig. Due to the drought, no one had harvested a crop in a decade. Due to lack of people healthy enough to work, houses were falling apart, mud walls eroding, reed roofs disintegrating. As parents died, children got passed to aunts and uncles until they died, then to grandmothers until they died, then to neighbors, then to the grandmothers of neighbors. Children lost track of where they were born and who their parents were. Some lost track of their own names. As they distanced themselves from their families and homesteads, they lost their inheritance of family homesteads. Old women found themselves with herds of children from unknown places, everyone sleeping on the floors of their little houses, sharing smoky air with people coughing up blood. No one in the world offered any help except the two old white women in the old Toyota, and they were lucky if they made it to half a dozen homesteads in a day, half a dozen out of 2,500 around St. Philip's.

At one homestead, apparently abandoned after the roof fell in, they looked around, found nobody. They asked a neighbor who said there was a small baby being cared for at the house by a "troubled" young girl and an old man. The sisters went back to the house, poked around, found a rib-skinny dog crouched beside a pile of rags. In the pile of rags they found a rib-skinny little boy named Menze. They picked him up. He didn't stir. He wasn't quite dead, but almost. The dog could have told them that. It was just waiting. The sisters took him back to the mission and nursed him back into life.

These people weren't just patients. Barbara and Diane developed close relationships with many of them. When they died, they were friends dying — hundreds and hundreds of friends. The sisters didn't cry much, but once in a while it happened. It happened to Diane the first time she got out of Swaziland. It was in 2006, after two years in-country. She went to a retreat in upstate New York, a place for prayer and contemplation. On the second day she got to contemplating about all the friends she'd seen die. She started sobbing and couldn't stop. She just sobbed and sobbed and sobbed.

Barbara sobbed when a girl named Tanzele died. Both of her parents had died, and she had HIV and tuberculosis. Twice a week she had to walk 19 kilometers to a clinic for medication. She was 13 when the sisters took her into the hostel. In the magical way of Swazis, she became happy. Everyone loved her. She took her medications and went to school every day. She giggled with the other girls. She played a game that involved dodging a ball of wadded-up plastic bags while trying to fill a soda bottle with sand. She was so proud of her excellent report card. When she went home to stay with relatives during a school break, she contracted measles.

Medical personnel and foreign aid workers didn't know what to do. They'd never seen anyone with HIV, TB, and measles. Barbara thought they didn't try hard enough to help her. When she died, Barbara wept — not just for the loss but for the fact of no one being able to save her. She wept for that and the reality that success had to be measured in such small increments. In Tanzele's case, it was a girl who was allowed to experience childhood for a few months.

There was hardly a day when either Diane or Barbara didn't decide to give up, to go home, to take on some other problem, one that could actually be solved. Every day was one day too much. But when they had time to stop and think about what they were doing, to relate their travails to Jesus, and to dispense with the notion of impossibility, they always managed to stay a little longer and go out to a few more homesteads to see what they could do. It's hard to walk away from people who are dying. In the dark of that strange and scary land, she realized that Dr. Hank didn't understand who the Missionary Sisters of Cabrini were and what they could accomplish when they felt it had to be done.

White Medicine in a Black World

People on the homesteads had no idea what was causing their maladies, which in a single individual were likely to include several sexually transmitted diseases. They might have tuberculosis that had spread from lungs to glands to bones. They often had Kaposi's sarcoma, a systemic viral infection that causes lesions on the skin, from soles to gums, down the gastrointestinal tract and into the lungs. They might have tumors under the arm, on the tongue, in the throat. They might have shingles as ugly and painful as a third-degree burn. They might have fungal growths down through the alimentary canal. They surely had chronic diarrhea. They had skin diseases Diane had never seen before. They had peripheral neuritis, an agonizing inflammation of the nerves of the lower leg. People in their twenties hobbled around like crippled elderly trying to keep their infected feet off the ground. Paranoid by the nature of their culture, they readily supposed they were the victims of a curse targeted at them as individuals. They didn't know how the disease spread, and when told, they didn't believe it. They believed what the "traditional healers" told them — that they had been cursed by a neighbor, that if the patient was a man, the prescribed cure might be sex with a virgin, or if the patient was a woman, the cure might be sex with the doctor himself. It might also involve little hash marks cut into the knuckles and other joints with a razor used on other people with the same medical complaint. Sometimes the healers, protective of their turf, told people to refuse the white medicine, that it would kill them.

The sisters recognized that they had to work within this culture. But they found it unfathomable. No one, not even the people they worked with, not even the ones with education and urban experience, was willing to offer more than a peek into its dark secrets. Ever since the English and Dutch colonization of the 19th century Swazis had learned to keep their African side veiled. The national motto, Siyinqaba, could be translated as "We are a fortress" but with the parallel meaning of "We are hidden; we are a mystery."

They spoke English with foreigners in a beautiful, off-kilter, almost poetic whisper, but they rarely said more than necessary. They answered open-ended questions with vague thoughts that seemed framed to tell the white people only what they wanted to hear. They answered yes-no questions honestly but with just one word. They were polite to the point of self-effacing humility. Women were reluctant to speak with men and afraid to speak with whites. When women came into the Cabrini clinic, they could not bring themselves to look at Diane. They stood half bowed, half turned away, speaking in a timid hush. The treatment and prevention of HIV had to begin with basic education: getting women to stand straight and speak up, and not just to talk with Diane. They would have to stand straight and speak up to their doctors, their husbands, their chiefs, their sorceresses and witch doctors. But they were as comfortable doing this as American women would be singing operatic-style to all the men in their lives.

Behavior was inexplicable. People would get sick and frightened enough to come in for testing, but when they went home, they hit family problems. Their husbands wouldn't allow them to get treated. Or their sisters talked them out of it. Or their healers would offer a more traditional option. Or their preachers would tell them Jesus would heal them. One patient came in and said that her preacher had cured her. When he prayed over her, she could feel the moment she was healed. She didn't come back until she was almost dead. There was a staff member whose mother was a sorceress. He was a "default tracker" who excelled at going out into the outback to track down people who had stopped picking up medications. For three years he showed the symptoms of AIDS, but his mother refused to let him get tested. He died at the age of 35. They found him lying naked in a building, waiting for his spirit to return to his body. Then he couldn't be buried on his homestead because it was feared that the neighbors who had bewitched him with HIV would come dig up his bones to use for rituals.

As they grappled with the causes and prevention of HIV and orphanhood, they came to see how the culture itself was the crux of the problem. Women, especially those in rural areas, had no way to say no to sex. It didn't matter if the man was an uncle or someone else's husband or a stranger who happened to come along. It didn't matter if he was HIV-positive. Swazi culture instilled such submission in women that psychologically they could not bring themselves to resist sex. A girl might well be pushed into marriage as a young teen, especially if deflowered. Her father would be compensated for the loss by a payment of cattle. Depending on the girl's beauty, virtues, family connections, and extent of virginity, she could be worth ten or twenty cows, maybe more, maybe less. Her proposing groom would actually negotiate with her father, giving reasons why she wasn't worth as many cows as her father liked to think.

While women were submissive in sex, men were sexually unencumbered. Though a neighbor's wife was technically off limits, adultery was a matter of what one could get away with more than an issue of morality. An unmarried sister-in-law was fair game. Virginity was something to respect, but not out of concern for the girl. Rather, it was a matter of how many cows she was worth before and after. Once violated, she was obliged to marry. If the man already had a wife, well, now he had another, though it might cost him a few cows. The wives slept on the floor near their husband's bed. When he wanted to lie with one of them, he called her over. They had a special verb for that.

On the other hand, none of that is necessarily true. Swazi sexual mores are confusing, convoluted, and contradictory. Any non-Swazi claiming to understand it probably hasn't asked enough Swazis to explain it. Barbara and Diane certainly didn't understand it.

Alcohol aggravated the situation. Home-based bars, called *shebeens*, sold a cheap, sweet, creamy home-made hootch made from the amarula fruit. The fruit ripened in February. Everybody spent the next month or two drunk. Crime rose. Pregnancies increased. Disease spread. Dedicated alcoholics kept it up for the rest of the year. They hung around the *shebeen* all day, often leaving kids unattended at home. If the individual had TB, the close and palsy-walsy quarters of the *shebeen* facilitated its transmission. As the day's drinking built up, the benefits of condom usage got forgotten. Inebriation enhanced the beauty of the famished barflies, and desperation for another drink increased the acceptability of a man with money. If the individual was HIV-positive, which he or she probably was, the virus soon found its way into a nice, new bloodstream. And everybody took home some TB bacilli for the kids.

Pius Mamba, one of few willing to give the sisters a little insight into Swazi culture, defined sex as a matter of power exchanged for pleasure. Women lacked social and economic power and privilege—the privilege of sitting on a chair rather than on the ground, of learning a trade and earning their own bread, of owning land, of deciding whom they would marry and how many children they would have and whom their husbands would marry. Their power was pretty much limited to how easily they would provide the pleasure of sex. Mr. Mamba called it "transactional sex." Women gave sex to get something, be it food, a cell phone, a ride into town, or a withholding of violence. While psychologically they couldn't say no, they could set some conditions for yes. They could try to get what they could for what they had to do anyway. Though other Swazis weren't necessarily as cynical (or articulate) as Mr. Mamba, his explanation was credible. Sister Diane knew a woman who was having sex with a man she knew to be HIV-positive. Her justification: "I'd rather die later with a full stomach than die hungry now."

Culture was at the root of the problem, but Barbara and Diane hadn't come to Swaziland to cure culture. They weren't even there to push Catholicism. Not exactly, not that directly. Yes, they believed the world was better off where Catholicism and its values were a way of life; yes, they would like to see more of it in Swaziland; no, they were not pushing it on people. They did not engage in catechism. Their mission was health care and child care. Yes, they led their children in Catholic prayer and Catholic song. Yes, they took their children to mass every Sunday. But aside from religious guidance for the children in the hostel, the sisters were bringing the love of Jesus to the local people not by thumping a Bible but by providing example. As Diane put it, they were in circumstances where they were better off living the love of God than talking about it. They were teaching by doing, nurturing love by loving.

But the frustration of working with an incorrigible and uncooperative culture gave rise to anger. sisters aren't supposed to experience anger, and they certainly aren't supposed to show it, but it happened. Like all sisters and nuns who struggle with the world's intractable problems, Barbara and Diane have a certain fire in them. Without that fire, they wouldn't be able to do what they do. They probably wouldn't even try. It's a good fire, but like all fire, it can burn. There were times when they lost control and lashed out at somebody too stupid or sluggish to see what needed to be done. The negative impression left by these incidents would haunt them for years.

And they lashed out at each other, an inevitability when two people

19

are exhausted and trying to solve problems which neither have seen before and which have no obvious solutions. But they were brief arguments free of ego or suspicion. They were both trying to accomplish the same thing, and they never had time for a drawn-out debate. They also understood the inevitability of failures along the way. Though a good deal of the time they didn't know what they were doing, at least they were doing something. Their failures were no worse than the default situation.

Toward the end of 2004, just months after the sisters arrived in Swaziland, the first free anti-retrovirals (ARVs) came into the country courtesy of the Global Fund to Fight AIDS, Tuberculosis and Malaria. At the same time, the President's Emergency Plan for AIDS Relief (PEPFAR), initiated by George W. Bush, started providing financial and technical assistance for promoting capacity, competence, and sustainability. The Global Fund was funded by donations from governments, the private sector, philanthropic organizations and individuals. The Bill and Melinda Gates Foundation was the largest non-governmental donor. The Global Fund provided (and carefully monitored) grants to governments to pay for medications and other materials.

In their first years dealing with the epidemic, the sisters could offer nothing more than access to health care — the blood tests, the rides to the hospital, the education. Columbia University's International Center for AIDS Care and Treatment Programs (ICAP) came to St. Philip's to help help raise the capacity of their local organization, Cabrini Ministries. Cabrini turned over its general clinic to the Severite Sisters, a diocesan order located at St. Philip's. On the next day, Cabrini opened a clinic dedicated to HIV/AIDS and TB. Big mistake. Because it was a new clinic, it had to go through all the government certification procedures again. But in time, as they increased their capacity, they would be able to test for HIV and TB and initiate treatments, avoiding the trips to Good Shepherd.

Anti-retrovirals, it turned out, worked better than sex with virgins and witch doctors. They didn't cure, but if combined with good nutrition, and if other illnesses were dealt with, ARVs could support immune systems enough for them to avoid the diseases associated with AIDS, prolonging life for more than a decade. They drastically reduced transmission of the virus through sex, and they could prevent contagion of newborns by their HIV-positive mothers.

In 2007, after knocking on innumerable doors and filing innumerable forms and beseeching innumerable government ministers and other officials, quite innocently neglecting to bribe everyone along the way, they got Cabrini Ministries registered as a not-for-profit. Around about that time, they gained a reputation for not only getting things done but implementing new programs quickly. They had no organizational bureaucracy holding them back, and they were far enough out in the sticks to be overlooked by the government. They became a model for how to most efficiently and effectively implement new projects. Ironically, they were still flying by the seat of their calf-length skirts, figuring things out as they charged forward, finding solutions for impossible problems and moving on.

By this point, average life expectancy in Swaziland was edging down toward 32 years, probably lower in the Lubombo region. The national population was declining, something that had rarely happened anywhere on earth since the bubonic plague hit Europe in the 14th century.

Though working in a place dense with disease, the sisters themselves had no time to be sick. They had to be in a lot of places at the same time. Mbabane was in the northwest corner of the country. Good Shepherd hospital was in Siteki, in the northeast corner of the country. Manzini was in the center of the country. St. Philip's was in the southeast. They had to move patients, medications, and blood samples to most of these places almost every day. They had to buy food in Manzini for the homesteads because the medications certainly weren't going to work on people who were starving. They had to divvy the food up into packages for delivery. They had to keep track of who had to go back to the hospital, who had children not being taken care of, who was failing to take their medications.

In the middle of all this, they were raising over a hundred traumatized children who needed a consistent supply of food, clothes, showers, and school materials. They needed warm words of encouragement in a cold, discouraging world. They needed admonishments for the gaffes and misdemeanors of childhood. They needed someone to explain the facts of life to them, including the fact that sex was synonymous with death. Their hostel needed a poster depicting a young, happy, hip-looking black woman saying, "I can live without sex."

The sisters had to teach people, one by one, why they had to continue medication once they'd started. They had to deal with the people they found on their porch every morning. They had to drive a full car past desperate people waving their hands weakly in hopes of a ride. They had to keep the car from falling apart. They had to dig it out of the sand or push it out of the mud or find a tractor to haul it out of the river. They had to rush people to the clinic with snake bites. They had to triage children to decide who was most likely to die if they didn't get into the hostel. They stopped everything to pray with people as they withered from the earth.

To avoid operating an ad hoc HIV clinic on their front porch, they set up a slightly more formal clinic in an empty room that belonged to the parish. Medical equipment wasn't much more than a couple of plastic tables and a few chairs. The examination room and waiting room shared the same open space. They had no pharmacy, no medications to dispense. In hot weather they moved a plastic table out front.

They couldn't resist last requests. They bought meat for an old man who craved that little luxury before he died. They bought coffins for people. When a dying woman requested a Coca-cola, Diane drove almost 100 km down dirt roads to get her one. Barbara said that wasn't a cost-effective use of gasoline and time. Diane said suppose it was your mother. Barbara then remembered what they were doing in Swaziland. It wasn't just health care and child care. It was compassion. They were there to love — to love and to show love, to show that it's all right to love your neighbor, that love can make life better. The siSwati language didn't even have a word for this kind of love.

Death by death they came to learn that they were dealing with values beyond their understanding. The basic human values they had always assumed innate to all humans were just Judeo-Christian values not necessarily shared by all cultures. They noticed that there were no Down Syndrome children, no children with cleft palates, no congenital deformities whatsoever. But an unusual number of newborns accidentally died while their mothers were washing clothes at the river — drowned, eaten by a crocodile, bitten by a mamba, or meeting some other euphemistic demise. Mothers were capable of infanticide, something the sisters had simply presumed beyond the instinct of mothers. Even more inexplicably, many people seemed unconcerned with their own survival. The urge to live wasn't present in everyone, and neither was the urge to let-live.

The sisters couldn't conclude whether this disregard for the most fundamental values was part of the old culture or a new-born product of trauma and poverty. The two overlapped. There was a young woman in their area, for example, whose parents died of AIDS when she was 14. That meant she'd been caring for them and the rest of the family for four or five years prior. Her adulthood had begun at about age ten. Soon after her parents died, she was raped and impregnated. She had a baby and at some point contracted HIV. She became pregnant again and endowed her newborn son with the gift of a deadly germ. The sisters met her when she was 20. She was taking her ARVs and giving them to her child, heading her household reasonably well. In fact, she seemed exceptionally intelligent and capable, so the sisters hired her to work in the clinic. They taught her to drive. Soon she got a job in a nearby town. But within a few weeks, she started to change. She didn't do her work. She argued with co-workers. She started alienating neighbors who had been trying to help her. She stopped taking her ARVs, and then she stopped giving them to her little boy. And then the little boy fell into a bucket of water and drowned. He was 11 months old.

Love and Death

As Barbara heard it, the girl had left the baby alone. There was a ten-liter bucket of water in the yard. The boy leaned over the bucket and fell in. But the story didn't ring true. The bucket was higher than the baby. Gravity couldn't pull a baby into it. And there were different stories about how the baby drowned. They didn't add up. As far as Barbara could determine, only God knew what had happened and understood what the girl had been going through. As Diane saw it, regardless of the details, it was a case like innumerable others — trauma and poverty pushing mothers beyond the realm of motherhood.

The baby's estranged father didn't want his son buried on his homestead. He and the girl weren't married, but since a child always belongs to the father, even if he's a rapist, it should have been buried on his homestead. The chief of the area, who by function of his position was supposed to straighten these situations out, refused to let her bury her child on her own homestead unless she paid him a thousand emalangeni, about $125, far more than she could ever come up with. The sisters made the payment, and the baby was finally put to rest where he belonged.

This cultural confluence of extended clans, sexual exploitation, gender inequality, quasi-feudal government structure, and self-serving morality had been working for many centuries. It might seem cruel, unfair, and inefficient to people raised in the presumptions of Judeo-Christian morality, but it worked to sustain the Swazi society. People reproduced and raised children to adulthood. Extended families took care of orphans and widows. Clans enforced the law. Chiefs and kings took care of politics. Polygamy worked to sustain the population and knit families together. Healers treated life's common illnesses. Society survived. But that cultural system worked only until HIV tossed a bomb into virtually every social institution — family, marriage, tradition, economy, health care, child care, community, education, land rights, and government. Whole families died. The links that held clans together were broken. The system of moral ity enforced by families and clans broke down. The traditional, socially regulated polygamy became an excuse for wanton sex that resulted in disease and babies but not families. Pubescent girls, unprotected by fathers and uncles, faced the inevitability of rape, pregnancy, infection, and infected babies. The loss of a generation of productive workers crippled the economy, and the cost of health programs drained the national treasury. The health system was overwhelmed. Schools were left without teachers, and children faced life with few professional or familial mentors to guide or protect them.

Diane and Barbara were applying love in a place that saw no use in it yet needed it with existential desperation. They didn't try to explain it, didn't push God on anybody, didn't try to draw an overt connection between the behavior-based plague and the tenets of the New Testament. They were simply applying love as best they could and hoping that people would catch on that the Christian kind of love could defeat the disease produced by the Swazi kind of love.

Sometimes the application of love involved the pursuit of bad snakes: Cobras that could spit venom ten feet. Pythons longer than that and big enough to swallow a goat. Black mambas. Green mambas. Puff adders half a foot thick. Puff adders account for more deaths in Africa than any other snake, but to Diane they aren't such a problem. They're slow. They stand their ground. Once you know where they are, you have time to kill them. But the mambas are quick and wiggly and a lot more lethal. Like puff adders and pythons, they can can be overhead in trees or underfoot along paths. When somebody screams about a snake, everybody comes running. They're so deadly that they cannot be allowed to escape. In their first six months in the country, the sisters killed a poisonous snake just about every week. One day a black mamba slithered into the house and into Diane's office. Diane did what Jesus would do. She went after it with a knobkierrie and smote the beast. A black mamba bit a thirteen-year-old boy. He died within an hour. The sisters' 150-pound Rhodesian ridgeback attacked a snake, got bit, and died within ten minutes. Its replacement, two lanky mutts named Boy and Socks, knew how to kill a snake, though they were reluctant to take on the ones that spit. They knew how to prance around a snake, pounce on it, snatch it up, bite it hard, give it a shake, fling it in the air before it could bite, pouncing again and again, two dogs and a pit viper playing cat and mouse. Everybody ran for cover until the flying snake lay still. Then Boy and Socks crouched beside it, bellies to the ground, watching.

Snakes don't wriggle over gravel, so the sisters' surrounded their house with a band of it. It was disturbing, then, to find a six-foot cobra on the porch in June on the evening of the Feast of the Sacred Heart. Snakes aren't active in June. It was winter. It couldn't have crawled there. Someone had delivered it. The Feast of the Sacred Heart happens to be a special day for Sisters of the Sacred Heart. The snake did not appear on that date by coincidence. No other snakes appeared inside the gravel zone until one arrived that same year on the evening of December 25. Both snakes were clearly a message even if the message wasn't clear. Was it a warning, an opinion, or a slap to the face of the Christian God, a response to the message of love?

Whatever it was, it didn't work. Nor did it happen again.

Applying love also meant loving a passel of orphans individually. There was no way to love them en masse. Each individual needed individual love. Each had inexpressible emotional baggage. Each needed vigilance and guidance down that rugged path toward becoming a loving human being. The path was especially rugged in Swaziland, of course, and even more so in Lubombo.

During the school year, the children under Cabrini's wing lived in two one-room dormitories, girls in one, boys in the other, about 60 in each, each more than half filled with bunk beds. Each morning at 5:30, everyone got up to take a shower and clean the place. An "auntie" in each dorm oversaw this remarkably disciplined and well organized process. The bunks were moved aside so a crew of assigned children could sweep the floor. They didn't argue with each other; they didn't talk back. They made their beds. They put on blue school uniforms. They shined their raggedy shoes. They combed their close-cropped hair. They ate a breakfast of cornmeal porridge and sour milk (it's supposed to be sour) cooked in big kettles over wood fires. They spooned it up with their fingers and then they washed their hands at a laundry sink in the yard. Before school they crowded around their auntie to receive pencils that had been broken in half so they'd last until the end of the school year. They ran to school when they heard the bell. They lined up outside, class by class, for twenty minutes of reminders that they were to shine their shoes, comb their hair, and not lose their pencils. They practiced saying the Lord's Prayer, phrase by phrase and class by class until their pronunciation pleased the director. Sometimes they were dispatched to gather firewood from nearby piles, fuel for the cooking of their lunch. When they went, they ran.

During school breaks, each went to a place like home. It might be the homestead of a parent or other relative. It might be the homestead of a *gogo* — any elderly woman who had a grandmotherly relationship with a child.

It might be that of an actual grandmother, but it could be a distant relative or a neighbor or the neighbor of a relative or the relative of a neighbor. Four siblings at the hostel had begun such a journey through homes after their mother died. Three of them were of one father, but the fourth was sure his father was someone else, though he didn't know who. When the father of the three died, the children moved in with a married sister. When her husband died, they all moved in with her in-laws. Her brother-in-law wanted to take the oldest girl as his wife. When she refused, the in-laws kicked all of them off the homestead. They moved from homestead to homestead but were unable to settle anywhere until a *gogo* took them in. No one knows how the *gogo* was related to them, whether by blood or friendship or just pity. When someone from St. Philip's went to visit them, the children said they hadn't eaten in two days. Their gogo, they said, had gone to look for a job so she could buy some food. But there are no jobs around St. Philip's, none at all. Food was less likely than starvation, so the four children were taken to the hostel.

Despite their orphanhood and roaming, all the children at the hostel had been at some point attached to a place and a person. The policy, therefore, was that the child needed to belong — to feel a sense of belonging — to a family and community. So that was where they went during school breaks. The sisters made sure they each took a bag of food staples with them so they weren't a burden on a family. They also checked up on families to make sure no one was being abused or going hungry. Not long after opening the hostel, the sisters realized that they couldn't take in every child who wanted a better place to live. They had to restrict admittance to the most desperate cases. Some of them were "double orphans" who had lost both parents. Some were "single orphans" whose remaining parent, probably sick and certainly poor, was unable to care for them. Consequently, each child at the hostel was suffering severe emotional trauma and very often such physical trauma as beatings, illness, hunger, and rape. Sexual trauma was not unusual and often undetectable. While most of their parents had died of AIDS, some had suffered something as mundane as being crushed in a car wreck or eaten by a crocodile. These weren't deaths in the distant sterility of a hospital. They happened at home. In the case of AIDS, they happened over the course of years on the floor of the only room in the house. Those left with one parent in all likelihood suffered hunger and neglect as the remaining parent almost inevitably wasted away of the same disease. Even if relatively healthy, that parent would be struggling to survive in a place of almost zero employment, little water or food, and a lot of extra kids around. UNICEF estimates that there are 100,000 of these children in Swaziland, a painful percentage in a country with a population that barely — and perhaps only temporarily — exceeds one million. The official term for these kids is "Orphaned and Vulnerable Children," a.k.a. OVCs.

Barbara wondered how a nation could raise a generation without any parents. She and Diane and her scant staff were just surrogate parents raising children for surrogate parents. They could provide only minimal care and love for only a thousandth of the OVCs in Swaziland. It was a hard, 24-7-365 job that had to be done carefully, with each individual, over the course of a decade or two. Virtually no one else was doing it. There were no government orphanages. In fact, the government denied the existence of orphans because the culture of the extended family supposedly embraced all children.

Textbooks distributed in Swaziland recognized the problem, but just a bit. They taught children that there were three kinds of families in the country: those with two parents, those with one parent, and those headed by a child. Barbara and Diane found that latter distinction downright offensive. A child cannot head a household. The notion was nothing more than government fantasy.

The sisters had to raise $3.29 a day to keep a given child fed, healthy, clothed, and loved. (To sponsor a child, go to http://www.cabriniministries. org/donate .) The Catholic Church, as a whole, does not fund the Missionary

Sisters of the Sacred Heart or any other congregation of women religious. Barbara and Diane had to find funding for everything they did. They pulled every string that connected them to people with money. They immediately spent whatever they raised. Nothing could wait. Children needed food every day. A vehicle without fuel could mean somebody dying. A wheel falling off a vehicle could mean a lot of people dying. When the old Ventura got too undependable for the transport of dying people, they hit up a friend for $25,000 for a new vehicle.

Then they discussed between themselves whether they should be taking the comfy new car with the nice new smell down the rocky, dusty, thorn-bordered trails of the outback to pick up sick people. Barbara suggested it be reserved for more civil trips. Diane asked which car she'd use to take her mother to the hospital. It was a question of efficiency versus humanity. And with no further discussion it was agreed that the nice new car would be used primarily for patients.

Then they got a $100,000 grant for an irrigation system. And then they wondered if it might be enough to produce potable tap water. The whole diocesan mission at St. Philip's — the elementary school, the high school, the hostel and clinic run by the diocese's Severite Sisters, the hostel and clinic that Barbara and Diane operated, the housing for the staff of these various operations — was using water pumped directly from the muddy, contaminated Usuthu river. The water was so dirty that pipes clogged with mud. It wasn't something a person would want to drink, though of course for lack of alternative everyone did. But a modern water system of municipal proportions wasn't something anybody could just go out and buy, not for $100,000 and certainly not in Swaziland.

Then one day a Zimbabwean named Peter Baker, a benefactor of the hostel, cogitated a possibility. He worked at a paint store in Manzini, but he revealed a secret expertise: water systems. He explained how a home-made system could extract filtered water from the river and deliver it to the mission. It was an impossible possibility, but theoretically it could be done. He was willing to offer his expertise. He came out to St. Philip's every weekend to explain each step. He drew pictures for a foreman, Esau. Esau couldn't read but was good at figuring out how to do things, in this case wall off part of the river, dig a vast hole six feet into the riverbed, line its outer perimeter with a filtering wall of stone packed into wire netting, then a wall of pebbles, then a wall of sand. This had to be done in the winter, when the river was low. The only machines were some sad, diesel-fueled pumps that labored day and night to keep some of the water out of the hole. The temperatures were in the 40s, and the men had to work wet. They had to find stones and lug them to the site. They had to dig up sand to make cement and mix the cement with shovels. They had to take orders from a nurse and a social worker who were really just figuring out how to build a municipal-sized water system with available materials and not much money. When the sisters saw the men laboring in the mud and water, they kept giving them raises without being asked. Before it was over, one man died of apparent pneumonia.

They had to build a pump house. They had to learn the mechanics of pumps and the physics of pumping. They had to explain to men how to install the pumps, then teach them to maintain the whole system. They had to learn about chlorine and aluminum. They had to lay pipe up to the mission, build towers for water tanks and then get the tanks up onto the towers. They had to get plumbing installed in buildings. It was a long, hard, impossible project. But once the whole thing got put together, they could open a tap and see clean water come out. They could drink it.

Not bad for a nurse (who at the same time was running a clinic during an epidemic), a social worker (overseeing the care of six score kids, some of them HIV-positive, all of them traumatized) and a bunch of men (some of them HIV-positive, all of them traumatized) who had never dug so much as a well. Such is the power of love.

But the love got complicated. The other organizations at St. Philip's mission — the schools, the Severite Sisters' hostel and clinic, the diocese itself — soon forgot that they'd promised to help pay for maintenance of the water system. The sisters kept paying for the whole thing, US$850 - 1,200 a month, money that could have funded eight to twelve children at the hostel. It wasn't fair, but what were they supposed to do, turn off everybody's water?

And so it went. Not much the sisters took on was anything they'd ever been trained to do, and the difficulties were compounded by Swaziland's lack of infrastructure and its people's lack of training and initiative. There were no construction companies to come in and build something. There were no trucks to deliver pre-mixed cement, no place to buy concrete blocks. Concrete blocks had to be made, but first molds had to be made, but before that somebody had to come up with lumber and nails and a hammer. Then somebody had to be taught that all the blocks had to be the same size, and then someone had to be taught the right way to build with concrete blocks. When the sisters hired Esau to build a house for visiting volunteers, he assured them he knew how. And did a pretty good job except that he neglected to make accommodations for plumbing and electricity, two niceties he'd never worked with.

Thus it was with all new staff. They had to begin learning from the most basic level. The only people in Swaziland with any skills beyond primitive agriculture and the weaving of reeds lived in a city. They were not inclined to move to Lubombo for any salary or any reason. The local people had never so much as used a telephone. They couldn't turn on a radio. Few could read or write. They didn't know what time it was or even what time was or even what time was for. Rare was the man who could drive a car.

Work, for people in Lubombo, had always been home-based and slo-mo, moving at the pace of seasons, not minutes. Family life and professional life were one and the same. People naturally assumed Cabrini operated the same way. They stood around talking a lot. They saw no problem with taking time off for a quickie down at the pump house. They brought inter-family squabbles to work. They threatened each other with death and cast spells on each other. The director of personnel, an intelligent, conscientious man invariably in a clean and well pressed button-down shirt, got bewitched so bad he had seizures in the office.

But training local people was part of the mission of child care and health care. To nurture life, the sisters had to nurture the economy of the region and the professional capacity of its people. The Cabrini Ministries board of directors — all of them Swazis — made a conscious decision to hire local people and to give hiring preference to HIV-positive candidates. They would avoid using foreign volunteers unless they were exceptionally and uniquely qualified. They would pay decent wages. This holistic approach was the only way that their work might extend beyond their stay in Swaziland.

Barbara and Diane were the only people in the country who were working this way — settling in to stay, employing local people, going directly to the ill, working with patients one-on-one, tracking their progress, and dealing with the holistic problem of illness, lack of food, orphaned children, decimated families, unemployment, and a dearth of medication, doctors, water, latrines, transportation, information, employment, technology, compassion, and hope. Benevolent organizations were busy all over southern Africa, but their results were rarely as good as their intentions. They unconsciously assumed they were working with people of culture and values similar to their own. They presumed that people would help each other, volunteer for their own communities, understand what they were told, take a little initiative, take advantage of opportunities in health and education. But these organizations and their people came and went. They rarely if ever stayed long enough to minimally understand the people they were dealing with. Typically, they would contribute the first part — the most visible part — of a long-term project. They might build a school, for example, then leave without finding, training, managing and funding staff. One organization arrived with thousands of tree seedlings. They organized people to plant them. But as soon as the organization left, the same people pulled up all the trees. Someone had told them the trees spread HIV.

Rekindling Hope

When I arrived in Swaziland in July of 2011, the country was nearly bankrupt, and for the first time in the nation's history, people were getting just a little restless. A so-called "April Uprising" hadn't amounted to much more than a brief riot quelled with enough police violence to make it not happen again, at least for for a while. By mid-winter — that would be August in Swaziland — teachers were on strike to protest salary cuts. A few weeks later, schools closed for lack of funding. When teachers converged on Manzini to protest, police pulled over passenger vans and sent them back if they contained teachers. Then lawyers went on strike to protest the corruption of the justice of the supreme court. Rowdy demonstrations in early September met violent police response. The calls for change then settled back to strikes and letters to the ditors of newspapers.

The country still led the world in HIV infection per capita. The Ministry of Health was maintaining that 26.1 percent of adults were HIV positive, but medical workers in the field, including Diane and Barbara, were sure the number was much higher. The only prevalence statistic considered accurate was the 42 percent for pregnant women. (The unique accuracy was possible since 97 percent of pregnant women were receiving prenatal care.) Since all of them were, by definition, sexually active and not protecting themselves, prevalence among the pregnant cohort was probably higher than that of the adult population as a whole. The overall mortality rate, however, was down thanks to the availability of ARV treatment for everyone who wanted it. Swaziland's population was growing again. To walk around Mbabane or Manzini, one would never suspect that at least one out of three or four people is HIV-positive.

I found St. Philip's at its apogee. Life was as good as it ever had been. For the first time in seven years, the sisters were able to slow down a bit. They didn't have a crisis every day. Problems, yes, of course, but problems that could be solved in time. They had seven vehicles on the road. The food supply for the children was pretty steady. Boy and Socks were doing a good job with the snakes. The clinic had just received certification to be a pharmacy. The water system was working as long as there was no power outage, which happened just about every day but rarely all day. Cabrini workers were putting the finishing touches on a comfortable new building for visiting volunteers. Diane said she started crying when she walked into it for the first time since the kitchen was put in, the tile floor laid out, everything looking so civilized. Seven years ago, she'd never imagined such a thing, really had never imagined much more than getting through another day.

It wasn't until the middle of 2011 that Sisters Barbara and Diane, representatives of the Catholic faith, realized they had to negotiate with witch doctors. Despite the presence of a health clinic and perfectly evident results of medication, people still put their faith in sorceresses who rolled bones to diagnose curses. They trusted healers who prescribed bizarre and dangerous remedies. When the medical professionals at the clinic told the sisters that they, too, respected the healers, the sisters realized they were still losing the struggle to change attitudes.

The time was ripe. A nurse named Jabalili who worked at Cabrini for 20 years also happened to be a traditional healer, a rather good one with a working knowledge of homeopathy. She offered to help. If Barbara and Diane could get permission from the local chief's "inner council," Jabalili would introduce the sisters to groups of healers and discuss the possibility of some kind of compromise or mutual effort. Jabalili would lead the discussion.

It had taken seven years to get to the point where a non-Swazi would be trusted enough to discuss this sensitive issue. It wasn't just a matter of health care. It was political. A shift from black magic to medication meant a shift in power. No one likes to give up power, especially not to white foreigners. That last time that had happened, in the 19th century when Swaziland invited the English to protect them from the Dutch, the results had not helped the local people. It was also going to be a radical shift in culture. The sisters knew that it was not going to happen easily or quickly. After seven years of dispensing medications and compassion, they were just being recognized, just a little bit, as offering something desirable, something good. And it wasn't just the care. It was the caring. It was also the logic, the reason.

"We want to tell the healers, hey, maybe your cures work for some things, but they don't work for HIV and TB," Barbara said as we rumbled down a dirt road toward a clinic in the foothills of the Lubombo mountains. "Our medicine works. You can see the results. But there is a deep spiritual side to Swazis. They believe in a mystical world and have a great desire to maintain that belief. We, on the other hand, are doing the corporal works of mercy — taking care of orphans, the sick, the impoverished."

Those plain, physical good works were bespeaking the value of hope, faith, charity, and good-ol' Christian love. Over the years, the staff at St. Philip's have come to understand this message, and they have changed. Today their communities see them as different. They are seen as people who will help not only on the mission but at home, good people, people who can be trusted not to poison a neighbor or cast a curse. This change,

Barbara says, may be one of Cabrini's most significant successes. The connection has been made between the corporal and the spiritual.

But in the battle for the children and against the virus, success has been elusive. In all the tales of tribulations I heard from the sisters, I saw tears only once, a sheen of glass in Barbara's blue eyes when she said, "In the end, we have failed."

That fundamental failure that lurks beneath innumerable and often intangible successes is the failure to stem the epidemic through education. For seven years the sisters have been pounding the basic message into the heads of their children — children who should be very receptive to warnings about what killed their parents. But of the 20 girls who have been raised to the age of graduating from high school, 18 have gotten pregnant. Five are already HIV positive. Now sexually active and in some cases already forced into marriage, the uninfected 13 are sure to be given the virus in the near future. The sisters are doing what they can to prevent the marriages until the girls get through high school and learn a trade, but in the continued risky behavior that led to the pregnancies, the sisters see the signs of another lost generation. The first generation died before it knew what was happening and learned how to prevent it. The second, it seems, knows but has not learned.

Sister Barbara was blazingly angry when a medical professional told kids at a Life Skills Camp that using birth control at a young age would make it harder to have babies later on. Barbara had specifically told the person not to repeat that absurd and lethal myth, but she did it anyway.

"We have kids becoming sexually active at the age of six," Barbara said. "We have eight-year-olds raping two-year-olds, without knowing what they're doing, of course, but they're doing it. And then a nurse tells teenagers not to use birth control."

According to the United Nations Programme on AIDS (UNAIDS), the number of children 14 years old or younger infected with HIV, based on Ministry of Health's questionable data, is rising. There were 13,106 existing cases reported in Swaziland in 2008, 14,320 in 2011. Some of the increase can be attributed to more ARV treatment and thus fewer deaths reducing the number of existing cases. The number of cases was projected to rise to 15,542 by 2015. AIDS deaths among children declined from 1,104 in 2008 to 806 in 2011 and are projected to drop to 308 in 2015.

The Cabrini clinic treats some seven or eight hundred unique patients each month. Since 2004 they have tested some 3,500 individuals. About half prove HIV-positive, a percentage that has been consistent throughout those years. The local rate of HIV-positive pregnancy is consistent with the 42 percent found for the rest of Swaziland. Despite the barrage of education, despite the free condoms everywhere from dispensers in public bathrooms to the cheerily decorated "Condobox" on the front desk of the Manzini public library, and despite the tempering effects of the ARVs, the rate of contagion has not diminished in Lubombo or anywhere else in the country.

Sister Barbara is tired of foreign reporters and activists asking why Cabrini Ministries isn't handing out condoms. Condom distribution, she says, isn't part of Cabrini's mission any more than praying with the dying is part of the Peace Corps mission. Cabrini educates people about condoms and tells them where they can get them. If they happen to get passed under the table at the clinic, the sisters aren't going to call down the wrath of God. Barbara's eyes fire up at the thought of people complaining about what Cabrini doesn't do.

"That kind of stuff drives us nuts," she says. "I want to tell these people, Hey, the Catholic Church isn't part of the problem in Swaziland; it's part of the solution. And who's doing more to solve the problem? Who really lives here and stays here and deals directly with the people who are dying?'"

She finds guidance in something Pope Benedict said while visiting Africa. He didn't identify abstinence or monogamy or condoms as the solution. He said that condoms are meaningless in Africa until sexuality becomes personal, loving, meaningful, and humanized. Barbara says that if she hadn't lived in Africa, she wouldn't have known what that meant. A male teacher at the school explained it to her. He said, "Sister, don't you understand? Swazi men are animals. We are like dogs."

"Now I would think that if I called you an animal because of your gender, that would be insulting to you," she told me, and she was right. "But it's not insulting to a Swazi man. He's not expected to have any impulse control over sex. Women will tell you that they have a choice about saying yes or no to a man, but in reality, they don't. Internally, psychologically, they can't say no. It's beyond the realm of their culture."

The sisters have had to tell their staff that it's not OK to have sex during working hours. The principal of the school left after being formally accused of having sex with students. It's widely acknowledged that it's not uncommon for teachers to be guilty of the same thing. (For the record, the school at St. Philip's is separate from Cabrini Ministries. The sisters have no control over it.) It's even common for priests in Swaziland to have lovers.

So condoms aren't going to solve the problem, not until sex is personal, loving, and meaningful. That is a cultural change so profound that even Jesus, in the person of two missionary sisters, is having a hard time making it happen. Nothing short of a miracle is going to make it happen in time. A culture can't change if its people are dead.

Swazis have not only resisted changing their behavior, but once infected, many still resist treatment. They still drag themselves in to the clinic with the late stages of the symptoms that so many of their relatives and neighbors have died of. Some still don't know what the problem is. Some aren't sure whether they want treatment, and, despite hours of consultation, they often decide they aren't ready. Some are still willing to let Jesus or witch doctors (or both) cast their magic cures. Some fear that the ARVs are a conspiracy of the white world to exterminate the black world. Some have immune systems so weak that the initial

ARV treatments make them sicker, so they stop. Some start treatment, feel better, and then stop. Stopping, of course, complicates subsequent treatment. The same problem occurs with people stopping TB treatment as soon as they feel better. Drug-resistant TB then evolves and takes hold. Continued mistreatment can lead to "extremely drug-resistant TB," which is expensive and difficult, if not impossible, to control. The cure for normal TB cost about $20-$25 per patient, a price that adds up for the 10,000 people treated each year. Multi-drug-resistant TB medications cost about twice that. Extremely drug-resistant TB medications cost $3,000 to $5,000 per patient. All forms can spread directly to healthy people — hosts. Good behavior doesn't prevent contagion. Inhaling is enough. It can happen in a crowded home or in public transportation. The staff at Cabrini fear it more than HIV.

Swaziland leads the world in not only per capita HIV but TB infections. Africa as a whole has 75 new cases of TB per annum per 100,000 people. Losotho, with the second highest national prevalence, has 600 new cases per 100,000. Swaziland has 1,274. Eighty-three percent of TB cases have HIV, which means TB treatment must be initiated before HIV treatment, and then the two treatments must be orchestrated carefully. Often side-effects of one treatment complicate or interrupt treatment of the other. TB in Swaziland was being cured about as fast as it was spreading. About 80 percent of the population is at least somewhat aware of TB, its causes, and the possibility of medical (as opposed to magical) treatment.

Dr. Kefas Samson, director of the World Health Organization's TB operation in Swaziland, says that Cabrini Ministries is a model for the rest of the country in its holistic program of education, detection, and treatment.

"I think Cabrini's involvement is very, very, very critical," he says. "When I came here in 2008, one of the key issues was that treatment outcomes were very, very poor. We tried to get at the root of the problem and find the solution. We found a very good model in what Cabrini is doing — actively following patients, knowing their names, knowing their homesteads, encouraging them to remain on treatment. We noted that Cabrini Ministries was having much better outcomes than other organizations. We advised the U.N. program to adopt the community-based model. And treatment outcomes are much better nationally. It may be a modest thing, but it's working."

Though Barbara and Diane have been in close contact with HIV, TB and the many other diseases associated with auto-immune deficiency, they have never contracted any. Diane says this is proof that they are diseases of poverty. They are far more likely to find a home in bodies that are malnourished and in other ways uncared for. Current nourishment and care aren't enough, she says. Staff members who were raised in poverty but now have enough food are still susceptible to TB. She thinks she and Barbara are relatively impervious to the germs because they are backed by a lifetime of good nourishment. By extension, the solution to the local health crisis should involve more than medications. It should involve eradication of poverty or at least adequate nutrition from infancy on.

The motto of Cabrini Ministries is "Restoring life. Rekindling hope." It's the moral umbrella over the innumerable people who were dying before they dragged themselves to the clinic. It reached to baby Menze being raised from near death beside his starving dog. It reached to a little boy named Ndoda, who was snatched from the jaws of a burial wrap. It reached to twins, Simo and Nosipho, 23 months old, the son and daughter of a woman named Nobuhle. She was suffering from alcoholism, dementia, HIV, and TB. She had the habit of leaving the twins in the care of her six-year-old while she went off drinking for days at a time. She was out of her mind. Cabrini had left the family a supply of Plumpinut, a nutritional supplement for children. As would be expected, the six-year-old had eaten it all. The twins' grandparents lived nearby, but they were alcoholic, too, and showing no concern for their youngest and obviously neglected grandchildren. When Cabrini staff found the twins, they were on the floor of their mother's dilapidated hut, alone and starving, just days from death. At an age when most children are running around with boundless energy, these two had yet to crawl or sit up. Their gaze was deadened and dull. The sisters rushed them to Good Shepherd, where they were fattened up for a couple of weeks. When they were brought back home, Cabrini's director of child care, Sharon Singleton, brought police and a government social worker to the scene. It was an amazing moment. No government worker had ever been to a homestead in that area, and the police had never shown interest in such matters. Sharon stood back and let them get as involved as possible. But their involvement went no deeper than to tell Nobuhle and her parents to take better care of the babies.

That clearly wasn't going to work. The twins were going to die. Barbara and Diane weren't sure what to do about it. Cabrini didn't take in infants, especially those who needed physical therapy. The hostel simply wasn't prepared for all the extra care. Overseeing 60 older boys or girls was already a lot for an auntie to oversee. (There was usually just one on duty for the girls, one for the boys.) Adding a baby to the job was a lot to ask.

But Cabrini Ministries' motto isn't "Ignoring Life." Barbara called a meeting of the child care staff. Half a dozen aunties and teachers set up chairs in a circle in the warm winter sun in the dirt yard outside the hostel. Barbara asked how they felt about taking on two infants. No one looked at her. One timidly mentioned diapers. But these were Swazi women. They weren't going to get vehement about anything. Before they could say no, Barbara slid into a prayerful speech about how they were being chosen by God at this crucial moment in history. She asked if anyone objected to bringing the twins to the hostel. No one said anything.

Cabrini was a bit short on drivers at the time, so I volunteered to drive a truck out to Nobuhle's homestead with Sharon Singleton. Sharon is incredibly meticulous in her vigilance over the children at the hostel. A Swazi orphan herself, she experienced a government orphanage, which is basically a temporary holding pen where kids stay until a relative is located. Sharon empathizes with her flock of Orphans and Vulnerable Children and has a sixth sense of what they need and the kind of trouble they can get into. No child passes her suspicious and loving eye without an inquiry into where they're going, who they're going with, what they plan to do. It seems that at any given moment, she knows where all her ten dozen children are and which of them are up to mischief. She knows not only all their names but all their family backgrounds — where they used to live, who their living relatives are, which children are step-siblings and distant cousins, what happened to their parents, and who's started "loving" a fellow OVC.

We drove down dirt roads along cane fields, then down smaller roads that became trails until the last trail became too clotted with brush. From there we climbed through one fence and over another, soon arriving at a couple of small, simple adobe houses and a shed of concrete blocks. There sat Nobuhle and her sister-in-law, hip to hip on a reed mat, legs extended straight out, backs impossibly straight, each of them weaving one side of a reed mat. The threads of it coiled around C-cell battery spools.

The awkward sitting posture is normal for women on rural homesteads. Only men are allowed to sit on something higher than ground level, and that was exactly what Nobuhle's elderly father was doing when we arrived. He looked permanently planted on a bucket and utterly unconcerned that his chickens were half starved, his dog famished, his garden abandoned, his women too lethargic to lift him out of poverty. Nobuhle's mother brought a mat for Sharon, a plastic jerry can for me. For a good half an hour, Sharon discussed what needed to be done and why. No one disagreed, but she wanted to make sure everyone understood and felt good about the twins being taken away for a while. It was understood that Nobuhle could see them when she comes to St. Philip's for her ARVs next Wednesday. On that same day, in fact, she could go meet with the representative from Family Life Services, an organization that distributes birth control devices. Everyone agreed that would be a good idea.

The next step was to drive half an hour out to Sipofaneni, the town where the dirt road from St. Philip's meets the highway, to talk with the government social worker. She was reluctant to agree to the plan. Sharon told her that she herself would call the social worker's office when it was time to take care of the burial of the twins. The day would surely come. The social worker then agreed that the twins could be taken to the hostel. So we bought some disposable diapers at a general store operated by gowned Muslim Indian immigrants and headed back to St. Philip's.

There we enlisted three high school girls from the hostel. One of them was the daughter of a man who was the brother of the father of the man reputedly the father of the twins. In the absence of any other family members, the twins were technically hers. That's how Swaziland manages to have no orphans. If necessary, they are parented by other orphans. The girls climbed in the back of an Isuzu pick-up with benches bolted to either side and a cap on top. I got in front with Zodwa, an administrator in the Cabrini office. Back at the homestead, Nobuhle was tipsy — not acting crazy but working her way into a bender. She had one twin on her hip. There was a lot of talk in siSwati that I couldn't understand, but it was obvious that no one was questioning the transfer. Nobuhle put the diapers on the twins, then handed them over to the high school girls. She was neither cold nor crying. For just a second, Nobuhle's eyes met mine. It was a long second, enough for me to see a certain prettiness in her tired, worn face, or maybe it was a prettiness that died a long time ago or that had never come to be. And maybe it was a second too long. Still looking at me, Nobuhle chattered something drunkenly. Everyone broke into the kind of laughter that caused people to hide their faces in their hands and peek between their fingers. Nobuhle had said she liked my looks and she wanted to love me.

She meant good-ol' Swazi love. But I hadn't brought any cows, so the best way to handle the situation was to hasten the twins away from the homestead, over one fence, through another, into the truck and back to the mission. There we found a crowd of kids waiting for us outside the hostel. Everybody wanted to see the twins. Sharon said to me, "They have come into such a big family." And indeed they had. Over the next few days, the twins were heavily dosed with affection from everyone, exactly what they needed in addition to food. But a few days later, they were diagnosed with TB. Just about everyone in the hostel and on the staff has been exposed with a hug, a cuddle, a nuzzle, or a kiss. Nonetheless — and this is a big testament to the holistic care the kids are getting — over the next few weeks no one seemed to be coming down with the disease. The effective prevention, it seemed, was good food, daily showers, a clean bed. And maybe love has something to do with it.

"Restoring Life" also refers to the mission's five hectare garden of cabbage, spinach, butternut squash and peri-peri peppers. Blessed with irrigation and some agricultural savoir faire, the garden is a productive green patch in a half-dead land. The cabbages are as large as the full embrace of the OVCs who come collect them for lunch. The peri-peris are sold to a Tabasco hot sauce factory. The kids pull weeds for a couple of hours every weekend, not for the labor of it but to teach them a bit of what they'd be learning if they lived on a homestead. Clinic patients help out, too, if they can, and they take home some of the crop.

When Barbara and Diane invited me to a Sunday afternoon spiritual reflection with a small group of American staff and visiting volunteers, they presented us with print-outs of Isaiah 58:6.

> This, rather, is the fasting I wish:
> Releasing those bound unjustly, untying the thongs of the
> yoke;
>> Set free the oppressed, breaking every yoke;
>> Sharing your bread with the hungry,
>> Sheltering the oppressed and the homeless;
>> Clothing the naked when you see them,
>> and not turning your back on your own.

Then your light shall break forth like the dawn,

and your wound shall quickly be healed;

Your vindication shall go before you

and the glory of the Lord shall be your rear guard.

Then you shall call, and the Lord will answer,

you shall cry for help, and he will say, Here I am!

If you remove from your midst oppression, false accusation

and malicious speech;

If you bestow your bread on the hungry and satisfy the

afflicted;

Then light shall rise for you in the darkness,

and the gloom shall become for you like midday;

Then the Lord will guide you always and give you plenty

even on parched land.

he will renew your strength, and you shall be like a watered

garden,

like a spring whose water never fails.

The passage could summarize the tenet behind Sisters Diane and Barbara as they work in the fast of a stark land, releasing people from the bonds of ignorance and poverty, sharing bread, sheltering the oppressed, clothing the naked, and not turning their backs on their own, their fellow human beings. And these people, enlightened and restored to life by love, shall be like a watered garden, a spring whose water never fails — heaven on an unforgiving earth.

The Dying Kingdom of an Uncaring King

Heaven on Earth is the plan, anyway. Progress in that direction has been limited yet priceless: Lives saved, children fed, children allowed a few years of childhood, inklings of new attitudes toward community and goodwill, and hope rekindled. But at the same time, "sheltering the oppressed" does not mean an end to oppression. The oppression in Swaziland may be expanding beyond matters of health and economics. The more typical oppression, plain political, threatens. The rumblings of unrest are being met with force rather than solutions. The government has not learned from history. It has overspent and over-borrowed and now hopes to forestall reality by smothering its harbingers.

Sister Barbara, having witnessed repression in Guatemala, says she can see it coming. She warned me to be careful. She'd just heard of an American who had been arrested for taking a picture of a Kentucky Fried Chicken billboard. Suspecting he was a foreign agitator, police held him for three hours. Other agitators, including protestors, might not be so lucky. In 2010, Prime Minister Barnabas Dlamini explicitly threatened protestors with sipakatane, a local form of torture involving the beating of bare feet with metal or wooden spikes. Barbara also wanted to make it very clear that Cabrini's mission in Swaziland does not include political activism. They do not get involved with unions or social justice or government reform. Their missions are a) health care, and b) child care. Period.

I received another warning at a lobola, a prenuptial ceremony at which a groom was formally handing over 17 cows for a fiancee with intricately braided hair, a big smile, rouged cheeks, and beaming eyes, well worth the whole herd. One of the cows was being barbecued and consumed by both families that day after a ceremonial slaughter effected with a spear inserted just so. The families eat separately, and men sit separate from women. I sat with the men of one side of the new family under a tree behind the Protestant church where the ceremony had begun. The host brought us a plastic pitcher of sour milk. To prove it wasn't poisoned, he took a symbolic sip before passing it into the circle of men. The conversation swayed between English, siSwati, and flat-out laughter childish in pitch and silliness. As the pitcher worked its way around the circle, I chatted with the young man next to me, easing the conversation to the realm of politics. He pursed his lips and inhaled and then quietly intimated that "in Swaziland, you can talk about anything, but if you touch politics, you will get burned."

But he talked about it anyway. His thoughts reflected the general opinion: The king is too far removed. He doesn't know what's happening to his subjects. His quasi-parliamentarian government is corrupt, expensive and negligent to the point of uselessness. The system needs to change before the country goes broke.

Under a constitution adopted in 2005, "the system" is a bicameral parliament under ultimate control of the king. The king appoints twenty senators, at least half of them women. Ten are appointed by the House of Assembly. In the assembly, 55 are elected from as many jurisdictions, four women are elected from each of the country's four regions, and ten other representatives are appointed by the king. The prime minister, appointed by the king, is an ex officio member of the assembly. The king holds the power to veto any legislative decision. A parallel system of rule, called tinkhundla, enlists the loyalty of a vast web of family members and beneficiaries. The king nourishes them and their loyalty with jobs, perquisites, and cash. They return the favor with political support and an acceptance of the status quo. It distributes assets through the economy but it's tough on the treasury and unrewarding to productivity. It's an expensive system of government that delivers little benefit to those who haven't grabbed hold of the tinkhundla teat. The International Monetary Fund estimates that the government payroll accounts for 18 percent of Swaziland's gross national product. Such a system cannot sustain itself. Its end is near, but nothing's ready to replace it.

Swaziland's newspapers, though risibly shoddy in reportage, have been bold enough to print letters and opinion pieces decrying government corruption and royal inaction. In among articles on rape, murder, microdisasters, and love affairs, articles quote officials warning of impending crises — national bankruptcy, predicted shortages of food and ARVs, wage cuts for government employees, the consequences of bungled this and that, a king with no sympathy for his people's worsening problems, a regal father who does not love them they way they love him.

And they do love him. They've always had a king, and he always saw to the country's basic needs (after, of course, his own rather expensive needs). The king is synonymous with the kingdom, its history, and its culture. No polls have ever been taken, but in all probability, most Swazis want a king. For the first time in Swazi history, however, they don't want the king they have. They want a good king. And an increasing number of people suggest that democracy might work better than a king who's asleep at the wheel.

In matters of sex (and just about everything else) King Mswati sets a bad example. He has 13 wives (down from 14 after one got caught in bed with his minister of justice), then only 12 (after one reportedly moved out in May of 2012 and disappeared, alleging years of emotional and physical abuse, a claim other ex-wives had made), each with her own palace and BMW. One of them (the one accused of bedding the minister of justice) was a sixteen-year-old Miss Teenage Swaziland when he wooed her. In 2001, he invoked a traditional law that required chastity of all girls until age 21 and had them wear tassels to signal their virginity. Any man who violated the law was to be fined one cow or the emalangeni equivalent of USD$ 152. Just weeks later, to the embarrassment of his kingdom, he took an under-aged girl as his eighth wife and forked over the retributive cow. Within a year, he revoked the law. He has refused to be tested for HIV or even to appear, for publicity purposes, as if he's being tested. And 14 wives aren't enough to satisfy him. According to several sources, he frequents the University of Swaziland in Mbabane to pick up girls. People say that in all likelihood he is HIV positive, though this is merely conjecture based on his behavior. Statistically, a third of his wives and lovers are probably HIV positive, and if tradition holds true to his highly traditional office, he's been lax about protecting himself and those with whom he shares the regal pleasure.

From two sources who prefer to remain anonymous I heard about a case of infuriating regal insensitivity. Several people from Swaziland were invited to weeklong conference on HIV/AIDS in New York. King Mswati was there, too, to give a keynote speech. And who could be better for the job but the king of the place with the world's highest prevalence? But during the week, no one saw him. He arrived for his speech. But an American diplomat who was there reported that Mswati had been in Atlantic City all week, gambling and no doubt losing a lot of emalangeni that could have been put to better use.

Bheki Mukubu, editor of The Nation, the only publication in the country that openly, honestly, and consistently criticizes the government, has not been afraid to go after his king.

"He's having one, long, continuous party," Mukubu told me in his tight, cramped, cluttered third-floor walk-up office in downtown Mbabane. "He's living good. He's living large. He's living like a king because he is a king. Except I think he's taken his eye off the ball."

The ball is the kingdom that has been handed down to him through the Dlamini family since the 18th century. He won't be much of a king if his kingdom is bankrupt and his people are dead. All that stand between him and the 14th century are foreign loans and free ARVs. According to the United Nations, HIV threatens the long term survival of Swaziland as a nation. But he seems oblivious to the reality of the threat.

"We've reached the point where we know we can't rely on him to tell us what to do," Mukubu said. "We have to take responsibility even though that would raise new questions in itself. Like: Do we really need him? He should come up with a solution, and we literally believe he knows best. If this country collapses, it collapses on him."

The situation in Swaziland is so dire, so close to its national demise, that monarchic power, wielded wisely, might be just what the country needs to confront the existential emergency. Unfortunately, just when Swaziland needs a philosopher king, it has a high school dropout king whose pursuits resemble those of dropouts everywhere: cars, casinos, women, good times, material goods — pursuit of the now without concern for the later, the me without others. Just as the Swaziland population has declined to take on the responsibility of governing themselves, their king has failed to take on the responsibility of his office.

Whether or not King Mswati is spending his country's money or his own is a good question. It's hard to draw a line between the two. For one thing, the king's finances are a secret and the nation's finances are murky. For another, the king is deeply and widely invested in Swaziland's most profitable industries. Sugar is a big one. Mswati's most notable enterprise and singular accomplishment is Tibiyo Taka Ngwane, a holding company with interests in sugar, mining, properties, insurance, manufacturing, tourism, and a newspaper, The Swazi Observer. It also invests in socioeconomic development projects. To what extent these companies are favored by government policy and subsidy, and to what extent the king himself benefits, are unknown. The chief justice who brought on the strike by attorneys also decreed that just as the king cannot be sued, neither can any corporation in which which he has interest. Tibiyo is exempt from taxation.

Investments in sugar cane may be the latest bomb tossed into a Swazi institution. As recently as 2009 the scene around St. Philip's was one of parched scrub, dry grass, and the occasional cactus — just enough vegetation to keep a few cattle alive if they have free range over wide areas. But by 2011, the predominant scene was of cane fields, a sea of rustling green sprinkled generously by modern irrigation systems. But the green is deceptive. Though the desert blooms with dense fronds undulating in the breeze, the fields are supplanting people and pastures for a cash crop destined to sweeten southern African Coca-Cola syrup and contribute to European cavities.

The blooming of Lubombo is a massive infrastructure project fundamentally supported by a grant from the European Development Fund and financing from several international development banks. Two dams and a network of canals and irrigation pipes have been installed under the auspices of the Swaziland Water and Agricultural Development Enterprise (SWADE). A reservoir stores water from the rainy season, allowing the Usuthu River to flow through the dry season. Over 2,600 households are expected to benefit directly from the project.

SWADE's goal is to alleviate poverty by "transforming the local economy from subsistence farming to sustainable commercial agriculture." In the face of drought and hunger, that goal is at first blush laudable, but the transformation is also a disruption of the local way of life, which, given the agonies of the crumbling culture and unending drought, might not necessarily be such a bad idea. Nor is it necessarily a good idea. Once the economy has transformed as planned, farming will no longer be a family activity. More food will have to come from neighboring countries and be paid for with cash gleaned from cane. Men will have to offer their brides' fathers something other than cattle. People will swing machetes and hoes for a living, an exhausting and brutal way to earn one's daily bread. It's employment, but it's also dis-employment for subsistence farmers — more cash, less crop.

The plan might pan out if field workers are paid enough to buy what they used to grow, but that's an unlikely scenario given that the work will be sporadic, and the wages will be determined not by what people need to live but by the price of an international commodity that needs to be competitive. The cost of the water system will pay off for the local people if they get some of the water. Apparently some will and some won't. Most of it, by far, goes to the cane. Some of the people who lost their land received new plots and new houses of concrete walls and tin roofs. Some, on the other hand, didn't. As would be expected, fertile land was taken for cane, and homesteads were relocated to less productive terrain. People who still raise cattle now have less pasturage. Not figured into the cost of the project is the cost of dentistry. Not that dentists are actually available, but if they were, they'd have plenty of business. Within a year of the first harvest, Swazis' famously pearly smiles were rotting, and front teeth were breaking off.

I drove around the outback at the start of a school break, delivering OVCs and their sacks of food to the homesteads they called home. I asked a lot of people what they thought about the cane project. Not one person expressed optimism. No one had been asked if they wanted to participate in the project. They were simply informed that they were moving. Not everyone who lost a homestead gained a new one. People who hadn't been moved yet were being told not to bury anyone else on their homesteads, a tradition going back centuries. If they lived anywhere near a cane field, they had to get used to planes spraying pesticides on their homes. Not many people had seen the promised tap water. In one place, a spigot was made available for anyone willing to pay five emalangeni a year. No one was, so the spigot was locked up.

The main benefit people have been promised is a dividend from the eventual sale of the cane. Everyone who has been displaced by cane is entitled to a piece of the action, but none expect the action to amount to much. Swaziland just doesn't work that way. Everyone is expecting a pittance at most, and it will be years until the crop comes in and the pittance trickles down to the people who lost their land. Only then will they know what a good deal they got when they lost their land.

Elizabeth Steenkamp, an auntie at the hostel, tells a tale in many ways typical. Now nearing middle age, she is one of 41 siblings. Her husband has long since disappeared. Her step-daughter is having an affair with a priest. She is sheltering nine people in her little house. Only two of them are related to her. To pay for food and school fees, she does laundry, weaves plastic bags into floor mats, and does whatever else she can to raise a little money. Her house is surrounded by cane fields. She's been told to move but not been given land to move to or compensation so that she can build another house. Her yard receives more than usual visitations by snakes that have fled the cane fields. The planes that spray pesticides over the fields spray her house, too, though the dosage isn't enough to kill the diaspora of mosquitoes, let alone the emigration of snakes. She doesn't like any of this, but she says, "What can I do? I don't have any money." She's not sure whether she's in on the "shares" of the cane crop. She thinks everyone would be better off if the cane fields were used to plant food.

Barbara and Diane are not among the fans of the cane and water project, though the roads that follow the canals allow them to go over streams instead of through them. There's talk of pavement from St. Philip's out to the highway. Water is more widely distributed, but they're worried about the social impact of uprooted homesteads.

"I'm fearful that the sugar cane is going to make our area poorer rather than richer," Barbara said. "Neighbors get separated. The powerful become more powerful. In my years in Guatemala, I saw the same thing with the banana farms. People become serfs on their own land because they can never get ahead. They owe everything to the company store. They pay to sleep in barracks. They are robbed of the little piece of land and the dignity of saying, ‚ÄòThis is mine.'"

While the benefits of the cane — the water, the employment — are reflected in the price of sugar, the negative impacts — the loss of food production, the end of subsistence farming, the uprooting of family homesteads, the pesticides, the tooth decay, the snakes, the mosquitos — are not. The local people are expected to absorb these intangible and unquantifiable costs. But Barbara and Diane, the only people in the region capable of understanding that things don't have to be the way they are or go the way they're going, would like to see some of these disadvantages reflected in the cost of doing business in Lubombo. If the local people are going to subsidize operations by suffering, then maybe someone should be asking the sugar companies to subsidize the programs that relieve the suffering. The sisters just might do that if they ever get the time to take a break from raising 121 kids and bailing against an unrelenting tide of disease.

The cane project certainly hasn't helped Swaziland solve its national financial crisis. Uncomfortable with an empty treasury, King Mswati went begging around southern Africa. He managed to get a promise of a loan of $2.4 billion emalangeni (US$ 300 million) from South Africa, a quarter of what he asked for and enough only for a few months of goverment expenses. It was a loan, not a gift, and it had many strings attached, among them respect for political rights, a safe return for exiles, better controls over government finance, vague moves toward a democratic government, and a 5.55 percent interest rate.

But Mswati was unwilling agree to anything other than the interest rate. He insisted that the political strings be detached. South Africa refused. At the same time, the International Monetary Fund was refusing to make recommendations Swaziland needed to borrow money elsewhere. Appeals to the European Union have only brought criticism of Mbabane's lack of democratic and financial accountability. Mswati's minister of finance made a mysterious trip to Qatar but apparently brought home nothing, and no one is sure what he went there for.

Meanwhile, the world seems to be preparing to abandon Swaziland to its fate. In November of 2011, the Global Fund announced that it would not be funding new projects in its Round 11 cycle of investments, due to start in 2012. Since Swaziland had failed to apply for Global Fund contributions in Round 10, it is ineligible for Round 11. Unless the country or its many NGOs find funding elsewhere, the supply of ARVs will diminish steeply.

Part of the Global Fund's financial problems was a five percent ($50 million) decrease in the U.S. contribution in 2011. At the same time, the President's Emergency Plan for AIDS Relief funding may be in danger. Its current five-year plan commits support through fiscal year 2013, but Congress could cut funding at any time. The program as a whole will come under review in 2014. Needless to say, Congress is not in the mood for sending money to faraway lands. President Obama was criticized for putting $6.8 billion for PEPFAR in his 2011 budget.

Nobody knows what will happen if the supply of ARVs stops. Almost certainly the little kingdom would suffer an intractable epidemic, half or more of its population hobbling around on staffs, their throats blocked by tumors, their legs bursting with sarcoma, their bowels unable to hold anything, their children left to fend for themselves in a place of lethal reptiles and rampant rape. None of these people would be producing anything or caring for children or accomplishing anything besides lining up outside hospitals and clinics. Without ARVs, contagion would increase. A certain percentage — those who remain monogamous and protected from rape — would succeed in avoiding infection even in the absence of ARVs, but the disease would always be present. The quality of life in such a society is unimaginable. Many presume South Africa would absorb

Swaziland, but others ask why anyone would want such a place, or rather, such a people. In the absence of the South African solution, it is not unlikely that as the situation deteriorated, government would succumb to a coup instigated by anyone with a modicum of power. It's hard to imagine the situation improving after that.

A beautiful and unsettling realization has occurred to Barbara and Diane. Cabrini Ministries is more self-sustaining than the government of the nation. They are able to deliver food, education, transportation, and health care to their constituency. They can feed and house orphans. They are solvent; the government isn't. Granted, they depend on infusions of foreign aid, but so does the government. It is beautiful to realize what they are accomplishing but terrifying that their accomplishments are in a country that is failing. Success aboard a sinking ship doesn't count for much.

The metaphor of the sinking ship came up at the 24th annual meeting of the Coordinating Assembly of Non-governmental Organizations (CANGO) which I attended in Manzini. The main discussion was whether NGOs should be meddling in politics and trying to influence parliament. Some felt each organization should stick to its primary missions. Others believed that nothing would change until the government had changed. Though the discussion was intelligent and thoughtful, everyone in the room — some 25 or 30 well dressed Swazis and a couple of foreign whites — looked glum and without hope. They saw no solution or end to the national crises. CANGO itself was out of money, as were most of its member organizations. Members were dropping out. The chairperson, Mr. Comfort Mabuza, noted that some several representatives were absent out of fear after being followed and harassed by the king's men. Others couldn't afford the trip to Manzini.

Mabuza's official statement for the year was titled "CANGO's Fearful Journey — It's not for the faint-hearted." And it went downhill from there, starting with a metaphoric depiction of sailors abandoning a sinking ship.

From there it descended into images of blind citizens in a kingdom aflame. Mabuza reflected on King Mswati's expressed desire to see Swaziland achieve "First-World Status" even as hospitals were without medications, thousands lived in dire poverty, and "rampant looting and theft have become part of our culture within the government machinery....This is a country where abnormal has become normal." He exhorted his members to get off the fence, take political positions, and make an effort to force parliament to get serious. His conclusion came back to the metaphoric ship: "Courageous captains you cannot jump ship as yet — many lives are depended (sic) on you — This ship must sail on." Applause was polite, but no one seemed to be falling off any fences.

Though no one expressed the slightest optimism, everyone seemed to recognize that the NGOs' missions had never been more important. Those missions, in fact, added up to much of what good governments should do: prevent and cure disease, care for and educate children, train workers, promote economic development, protect rights, defend women, and promote adherence to law. Given the bankruptcy and dysfunction of the government, the NGOs just might end up being the de facto government — if they can survive the times.

Given the sustainability of Cabrini Ministries and and the array of 21st-century services offered by Swaziland's NGO's, I couldn't help but wonder if the little kingdom was poised between two brinks — one at the abyss of self-extermination, the other at the dawn of a new kind of government, a default government of organizations working independently and together to establish justice, ensure domestic tranquility, promote the general welfare, and secure the blessings of liberty for a people and their posterity. Would it be any worse than an uncaring king and a corrupt parliament?

But as 2011 rolled into 2012, the ship was still sinking. At St. Philip's, it was hard to say whether life had already been as good as it was going to get. The mortal struggle between the greatest achievement of life — the human spirit — and the tiniest form of life — the virus — was far from over. The Global Fund was scurrying to find a way to continue funding ARV and TB medications. Diane and Barbara were already presuming and preparing for a likely end or reduction of PEPFAR support. The government was no longer able to buy reagents needed for CD4 tests, so it was hard to determine who needed ARVs and how well treatment was working. At an army base outside of Manzini there were rumblings of discontent over food shortages, and soldiers sang a song calling for the ouster of the king. At St. Philip's, the issue of paying for the water treatment system by its several constituencies had not been resolved. Cabrini Ministries was still paying over US$ 1,000 a month to keep it running. The situation was getting more urgent because a tower that held water tanks was about to collapse. Government funding of the schools was increasingly sporadic. The Internet had arrived by G3, but it was slow and expensive, and blackouts were still common. One of Cabrini's seven vehicles had broken a frame, another was badly damaged in an accident, and another was wobbling through its last days and running up quite a bill as it went. The hostel had sponsorships for most of its children but still lacked about ten, and the waiting list was as long as ever. When Nobuhle came to visit her twins, she was visibly pregnant. As the weather warmed, several deadly snakes were killed not far from the hostel. One morning in early January, the sisters found a seven-foot black mamba, all chewed up, stretched across their driveway. Nearby, under a bush, the good dog Boy lay curled up, dead.

Acknowledgement

Special thanks go first and foremost to sisters Diane DalleMolle and Barbara Staley for all the time they took from their incredibly busy schedule to talk with me. Sharon Singleton also contributed much to my understanding, such as it is, of the Swazi culture and the workings of St. Philip's Mission. Thanks, too, for those who taught me so much at St. Philip's: Thandiwe, Esau, Zodwa, Mzamo, Mavis, Mr. and Mrs. Mamba, Themba, Johannes, Bongani, and Elizabeth. I thank Rev. Ken W. Jefferson for lots of good information. I thank Ben, Beth and Mikayla Kickert and Katie McCaskie for their friendship and their help with so many details, and I thank Denise Dembinski, Ian Cheney, Ralph Chney, and Richard Waterman for help with editing. Extra big thanks and a hug go to my wife, Solange Aurora Cavalcante Cheney, for her support with this project.

Sponsorship

To sponsor a child at the St. Philip's hostel, go to http://www. cabriniministries.org/donate. All of a sponsor's funds go directly to the support of a specific child whose progress reports are sent to sponsors. Contributions made through this site are tax deductible in the United States.

Sister Barbara Staley

Sr. Barbara Staley has been a Missionary Sister of the Sacred Heart since 1988. She has a bachelor's degree in Education from Clarion University of Pennsylvania and a Masters of Social York from New York University. She has worked with many poor and marginalized populations within the United States and abroad. Her work has included working with the developmentally disabled in residential care settings, providing counselling to street children in New York City, helping undocumented immigrants with accessing health care and social services in Chicago, providing mental health services to the mentally ill and to persons with addictions, activities of human promotion in Guatemala, and establishing a clinic in the outback of Swaziland to help persons with HIV, their families, and orphans.

Sister Barbara currently serves as the Superior General of her religious congregation. The organization of women religious, which has borne the missionary legacy of St. Frances Xavier Cabrini since 1880, is active in 15 countries on six continents. For more information, see mothercabrini. org or msccabrini.org. For more on Sr. Barbara's work in Swaziland, see Cabriniministries.org.

Glenn Alan Cheney

Glenn Alan Cheney is the author or translator of more than 25 books, hundreds of articles, and many an op-ed essay. His books, fiction and nonfiction for children, teens, and adults, are on such disparate topics as nuclear proliferation, Brazil's Quilombo dos Palmares (a 17th century nation of fugitive slaves), press accounts following the death of Abraham Lincoln, Mohandas Gandhi, atomic testing, television, Central American politics, the Pilgrims, Brazil, Bees, and Chernobyl. He also translates Portuguese to English. Most of his articles are about business, finance, and accounting. He holds degrees in philosophy, communication, English, and creative writing. Active in local politics, he has served on his town's board of selectmen, board of finance, inland wetlands commission, volunteer fire department, library board, and historical society. He lives in Hanover, Conn., with his wife, Solange.

47402201R00052

Made in the USA
Middletown, DE
24 August 2017